Waves of Lucidity

I will drown beneath
a beautiful canopy of stars;
it was meant to end,
just like this …
alone.

~Wayne Russell
(excerpt from "Alone" pg. 37)

Also, by Wayne Russell

Splinter of the Moon (Silver Bow Publishing 2023)
Where Angels Fear (Guarilia Genius Press 2020)

Waves
of Lucidity

Wayne Russell

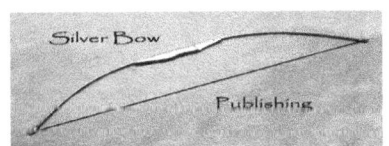

720 – Sixth Street, Box # 5
New Westminster, BC
V3C 3C5   CANADA

Waves of Lucidity

Title: Waves of Lucidity
Author: Wayne Russell
Publisher: Silver Bow Publishing
Cover Art: "Tranquility" painting by Candice James
Layout/Design/Editing: Candice James

All rights reserved including the right to reproduce or translate this book or any portions thereof, in any form without the permission of the publisher. Except for the use of short passages for review purposes, no part of this book may be reproduced, in part or in whole, or transmitted in any form or by any means, either by means electronically or mechanically, including photocopying, recording, or any information or storage retrieval system without prior permission in writing from the publisher.

ISBN: 978-1-77403-316-6 paperback
ISBN: 978-1-77403-317-3 e- book

© Silver Bow Publishing 2024

Library and Archives Canada Cataloguing in Publication

Title: Waves of lucidity / Wayne Russell.
Names: Russell, Wayne (Poet), author.
Identifiers: Canadiana (print) 20240434560 | Canadiana (ebook) 20240434609 | ISBN 9781774033166
   (softcover) | ISBN 9781774033173 (Kindle)
Subjects: LCGFT: Poetry.
Classification: LCC PS3618.U772 W38 2024 | DDC 811/.6—dc23

**For my children Chris and Gabi
with all my love**.

Waves of Lucidity

Acknowledgements:

I would like to thank my publisher Candice James at Silver Bow Publishing for her continued support and belief in my writing. I would like to thank my higher power in helping me navigate through this life, through the good times, as well as the most challenging ones. Thank you also to my two beautiful children and stepchildren, you have all greatly enhanced and been a blessing in my life. Thank you also to my beautiful, amazing, and fearlessly intelligent wife Jennifer, you continue to make me the most unbelievably luckiest guy in the world, much love to you always.

Waves of Lucidity

Contents

Waves of Lucidity / 11
Thunderstorm / 12
Just Believe / 13
In the Throes of a Perfect Exile / 14
Fleeting Images / 15
White Flowers / 16
Coin Toss / 17
Morning Mystery / 18
Checking Out / 20
There is Strength in Knowing / 21
Gazing / 22
Strength in Numbers / 23
Escape / 24
Ode / 25
Of a Lifetime / 26
The Painter on the Beach / 27
Grey / 28
From the Beginning / 29
Never Mind / 30
Desert Bloom / 31
Ocean Mist / 32
Memories of Driving / 33
Stratosphere Dreams / 34
There's a Plague Upon the Land / 35
Ethereal / 36
Being in Love / 37
Alone / 38
The Cardinal / 39
My Life With You / 40
Two Hearts / 41
Love Poem / 42
I Still Thin of Her, That Gulf of Mexico / 43
Thursday Night / 44
Cryptic Thoughts / 45
Manifest the Night / 46
The Ol' Mill / 47

The Dance / 48
The 8th of April Eclipse . / 49
Clear Blues / 50
Morning Songs / 51
Happy Anniversary / 52
Surreal Montage / 53
Your Song / 54
It's Summer Within Our Hearts / 55
Roses / 56
And Your Eyes Will See / 57
The Mere Thought of Us / 58
Secret Garden / 59
On Sundays / 60
You Are My Destiny / 61
Your Wilderness/62
Crossing Over / 63
Sad Café / 64
Release / 65
The Transient Old Man / 66
Cabin in the Woods / 67
Lady of the Cosmos / 68
Beat Down in Motor City / 69
When Life Was Our Song / 70
From the Ashes / 71

Author Profile / 72

Waves of Lucidity

The ocean cradles your soul,
rocking so gently, back and forth
like a clock's pendulum.
        Soothing,
like your voice softly whispering,

I run backwards into the womb of earth,
safely home, where it all began,
    blessed and kissed
by the mouth of fragrant stars.

Lie down here beside me.
Eternity is patiently waiting.

We'll ride upon an angels' wings
in the winter of this one life,
before we ascend, warm and basking,
in that golden glow of sunrise.

The Thunderstorm

Rolling thunder is drowning the night.
It's only been a few days away from you;
and yet those gnawing pangs of loneliness
have escalated in your absence.

I close my eyes and see your face,
hear your soft voice,
your whispers in my ear
lulling me into a sense of calm.
The thunder barrels
throughout a doom-laden sky;
you're miles away, an ocean apart,
choppy waves and angry skies separate us.

I can't wait to hold you again,
I can smell your perfume on your pillow,
I clutch it holding on tightly,
wishing it were you
        whispering sweetly into my ear,
              lulling me too sleep,
with the sound of the rolling thunder
playing like a scratched record
        off in the distance,
like the music soundtrack of our lives
    receding into the sweetness
      of long overdue sleep.

Just Believe

Enveloped in green
silken allure of pale leaves,
the rough faded brown texture of bark.

The bushy-tailed, brown-coated squirrels,
hyper and scampering, as always,
agents on secret missions.

Being back home again,
I stare out the streaked windows
at an ominous red-brick walled wilderness-
questioning everything in my thought process:
      What is this all about?
      What is it for ... this life?

The stock dove coos outside my window,
a small angel with delicate wings,
calmly assuring me that everything
will someday be revealed.

In the Throes of a Perfect Exile

Where am I,
ghost of bedraggled sky?
Hazy mist, lost in mountain crescendo,
shards of green exist here in Swiss exile.

I would like to rest here,
I would allow my stark-naked bones
to rattle in the breeze.

Let those dark birds in the snow cry;
let them envelope our aura
with a shrill death rattle song.

Where am I?
There's nothing in my way now.
There's no time nagging with his hands,
old as a sundial in ancient times,
no shadows lurking, no one looking.

Fleeting Images

Fleeting images
jostling for a permanent place
in the hallowed halls of my mind,
can't help drowning in my nostalgia.

I hold her safely within
the sweaty palm of my hand,
the soul of this candle trembling
in the gentle Springtime breeze.

The river continues its journey
effortlessly, lost in the haze
    of millennia gone;

I can see her in dark shadows,
    her ghost drifting
in the abstract of life, death
and everything else in-between.

White Flowers

White flowers in a vase
symbolizing my love for you,
    not as beautiful
  or magnificent as you;
  not as breathtaking
    or radiant as you.

But it is here they stand
in their clear vase,
awaiting your return like I do.

Every time you have to go away,
    I stand alone,
  looking at white flowers
    in a clear vase.

    I sigh and carry on
with all the mundane task of life,
    with thoughts of you
etched into the corridors of my mind.

Coin Toss

Night felt dead in her own skin,
only feeling alive with the elixir
of moonbeams reflecting
off the Seine River in Paris.

Twinkling lights that bedazzled
the Eiffel Tower five minutes
every hour from 8 PM to 1 AM,
making even the most downtrodden
feel alive, if only for a while.

Hearing those voices echoing
in the busy winds of the Parisian Spring,
those artist and poets, those troubadours
basking underneath phosphorus stars,
the alive and dead both wide eyed
like children in a candy store.

Lost souls swimming in the magic
of the eternal city of love and of heartache,
it's a coin toss here,
choose a side
and flip the coin.

Morning Mystery

We strolled into the bar on Victor Hugo Avenue,
not too far from the Arc De Triumph.

The barkeep was simply nowhere to be found,
we peered into the abyss of bottles,
and our mirrored reflections
were half puzzled half amused.

We sauntered outside
and sat in little rickety chairs
at a tiny round table.
We were relieved
to at least be able to rest,
if only for the moment.

We started making small talk
between our amused chuckles.
I adore you always,
when you're making plans.
You're so amazingly brilliant
in everything you do,
so methodically clever.

I loved just sitting there,
lost in the moment, at that bar
waiting for the barkeep to take out orders.

I loved watching the wheels turn
in your brilliant mind
as the clouds built
and traffic grew frantic in the morning.

Finally, I heard a voice
and it broke my train of thought.
You saw his face first, then me;
he appeared out of nowhere.

So politely, he sheepishly apologized
for his missing in action status.

May I take your orders Madam, Monsieur?

We agreed it would be crepes
and coffees all around.

Checking Out

As he checked out from that roach motel
on a remote stretch of beach front wilderness,
the sun was still yawning, raising and shining,
a slow burn like a shot of scotch.

He was clean but still unshaven.
The cracked asphalt of lonely highway
never complained. His ex-wife used to,
but that was over years ago;
it didn't matter anymore, nothing does.

He's a writer and a life wrecker,
leaving pain and destruction
wherever he may roam.

The keys of his Harley hit the ignition,
he feels the pangs of loneliness,
the key is turned, he starts down
the stench of lonely highway,
last night's whiskey
and today's cologne intermingling,
with the motorcycle's exhaust.

The roar of the engine helps drown out
the silence of his life of solitude.
He guns the gas and disappears
down a lonely stretch of highway,
over the horizon he rides
into the new glistening day born anew.

There is Strength in Knowing

I sit in a royal blue chair.
It has wooden armrests.
The tiles are yellowed with age;
they used to be as white
as those of the asylum.

The walls are cinder blocks,
ducks in a row, all painted white;
they too yellow with the passing of time.

I am alone and await the hour
when time dictates I must feed
that nasty machine.

There's work that must be done.
I wander these halls of loneliness.
For a pittance I work, hidden away
from society, toiling in the night;
my depression says run!

There's a bridge by the old asylum,
where the cherry blossom trees
bow at the foot of muddy normalcy.

There is a freedom in knowing, ultimately,
I hold the key to this rusted old cage
and I can fly away from this anytime.

Gazing

You stood outside —
I stood in awe,
quietly gazing
through the haze
of a night vision window,
watching you graze on
the freshly mowed lawn.

Alas,
you could sense
danger closing in
on all sides.
Fight or flight kicking in —

The drunken college kid
on a bicycle approached you —
so off into the rain slicked night
you ran, never knowing
the awe you inspired.

Strength in Numbers

There's a tunnel in the small town
of Zaleski, Ohio; rumor has it that it's haunted.

I've been there in the daytime,
but even though I don't believe in ghosts,
I wouldn't want to be out there alone, at night.
Alone with the skin crawling howling of wolves
and the hooting of monotoned owls.
Fruit bats have been seen clumsily-flying
around the entrance to the tunnel.

There're other bridges,
relics of a bygone era, and a campsite
where you can drink beer and whiskey
from Uncle Bucks Stable and Dance Hall.

You can pop a tent and light a small campfire.
You can wash the lonely hours away with alcohol
or tell scary stories to whoever is with you.

They say that out in the woods late at night,
evanescent forms and ghouls haunt that place,
        and as for me,
    I would definitely keep my trips
to Moonville Tunnel confined to my daylight hours
        and use the "buddy system"

        I've been told
     there's strength in numbers.

Escape

Summer swelter may be here,
lost in thickets and brambles,
the birds are informative in
mode of songs sung.

Lushness of the forest
and lawns, yellow green in hue,
sorrow is melting away
and rocks and stones
align sacred grounds,
hallowed and forming pyres
and worship sites of elders gone before,
drifting with the spirits of nautical nights
hoisting the anchor and setting sail
into the fathomed wilderness
of an oceanside shanty escape.

Ode

Summer moved on —
The lover's strolled beaches,
from youth into twilight years —

only to be parted by
the cruel hands of death,
now stopped.

And by the circling hands
of time, beginning again,
beginning again, a calm
transition from flesh and blood
into spirits soaring with seagulls.

Memories in photos left behind,
tattered and worn
those memories lie silent
basking in a sun kissed era
fading into —

a last breath passed,
a whispering and eternal
ode of love to thee.

Of a Lifetime

Cast me back into the Belfast night,
lay your warm kisses
at the base of my neck-
the warmth of your sighs
and yearning of your soul,
kiss the infusion of ocean myth,
oh my dearest angel, my only love-
I'll be there like a Celtic song,
I'll always be waiting for you,
in the Springtime of our life-
        and
in the darkness and disparity of death
that shall ultimately wrench us apart,
     do not mourn,
for this is the ocean fathomed
in her mild cloak, it wasn't for us,
enough rapture in the world,
set free on the footpaths of melting sands;
set free on the illustrious wings of heavenly will.

The Painter on the Beach

Woman on the beach
painting in oil pastels,
the day is warm and
turns her shoulders,
neck and face red.
Undeterred she continues
underneath an umbrella blue sky.

The seafowl sing just for her,
the pictures are taking form now
    for all the world to see.
Bold dark lines housing bronze,
     spirit eye shimmering,
        A sage?
        A medicine man?

Only the painter knows the story
of her beautiful creation,
yet, she holds a vow of silence,
running to the beach electing instead
to dance in the sands-of ebb & flow
        a portal of time
        bequeathed to
          the gods of
            serenity.

Grey

The visceral cortex of a universe gone mad,
the cerebral grey folds of skies
refusing to unfurl.

Here we are now, vanquished,
trapped in this mortal coil,
but it's not for long
and soon that grey silence
of slate, marble tomb
shall swallow our mute entity.

We shall be sealed over and forgotten,
an ocean wave collapsed,
driven silent upon the shore,
where stars are hidden
by the grey hand of God.

From the Beginning

There's a quiet storm
brewing in the streets tonight,
a million years of rage
now simmered to a boil.

Everything has come to pass,
the homeless man sleeps on a park bench,
the plastic bag blows past him
in the angry breeze
like a sad contemporary tumbleweed
awaiting the apocalypse
that's been coming
since the beginning of time.

Never Mind

The birds are lost and confused
       in their chatter;
     springtime pollen
     like yellow cocaine
into the abyss of nasal passages.

Nursing a hangover
with coffee this morning
I shall look back on this gathering
with a blurred vision.

Never mind the streets and highways,
Never mind the ravenous birds
that hover above.

Desert Bloom

Your earth is rare.
Shoe leather gaze
on the tired sky.
Cracked earth
in mock surrender.

You should be
the one rejoicing.
You should be
the one in bloom,
but your weary veins
refuse to pump life's blood.

You're just too tired
and worn to continue.

Ocean Mist

I've heard the material things in life
are a consumerist grift.

They are loaned to us only a little while.
When we die, or retire to the scrap heap,
those items must be returned,
.

       In a perfect world,
I would look out the sea salted window
of a boathouse in Laugharne, Wales
      like Thomas did.

I'd listen to the high lonesome cries
of seafowl the ominous crashing of waves
opening the craggy shorelines
   of the imagination
and write me into legendary status,
venturing into that gentle good night,
     way too soon,
even though I was warned not to go.

Memories of Driving

A slow drive down the winding roads
at the end of the world
to a rocky shoreline down below.
There is a massive drop.
That first step would be a doozy.

A perpetual dark green tapestry,
The greys of cliffs and steep drops.

The murky ominous Pacific;
a strategic mystery unravels,
beneath its depths.

Vines climbing up
towards the long white clouds,
winds serenade the jade ferns
and the tui birds shouting their name
in steep repetition.

I am unable to see those flightless birds,
that kiwi that hides in its nocturnal cocoon
of slumber.

I am unable to see that flowing hillside
jade palace of exile, and yet,
in stark contrast —
we are leaving this place,
in a dream that softly unfurls,
while life here abruptly continues.

Stratosphere Dreams

stratosphere dreams
sand running through
fingers of a vast universe
let's be an architect
and construct an uncharted realm,
a brave mythology that soars
on sound frequencies above
translucent angels bowing
towards the fragrant dandelion
     stars, you're the one,
       my only muse,
    my thoughts always
drifting backwards into your arms,
those large cool pools of blue,
  singing soothing lullabies;
      rest my love,
  dreams shall free us.

There's a Plague Upon the Land

There's a plague upon the land,
yellow monsters on the prowl,
mangled torsos thrust,
strong arms outstretched and then
clutching onto anything in their path.

Can you hear the voices of the elder's cry?
And just who gave you the right
to exploit this once vast land,
to desecrate this yellow moon rising,
to replace people's, culture's
and their way of life?

The land and people have been stripped bare,
wolves howling in the distance,
the golden medallion sun
has been obscured by the dust cast up,
by those yellow monsters,
and into the eyes of once blue skies.

I can hear the river sigh,
the birds' hearts beating
with quick rhythm of broken wings,
I can hear reverberating thunder,
mock star surrender,
through the vines and tree lines.

There's a plague upon the land,
reap the naked harvest while you can
Hillsides surrender
to all things of grey and greed,
now we transpire into the abyss
of that dark green cloak of money,
that wears a ragged papyrus veil.

Ethereal

ethereal tapestry
poetry in descent
such as mythical universe
caught between the rising spires
of the surreal kingdom
a complexity longing for only truth
the wisdom is trapped within
we already know one another
we already have encapsulated
this mind enhanced sphere.

Being in Love

It may seem cliche
a thunderbolt that hit me,
first date, head over heels
in love with her.

That whirlwind romance,
feeling enamored like a child,
for the first time ever.

That dream wedding day;
friends and family gathered
and the woman of my dreams
that said I do.

Is this the real thing?
The glowing of my soul
says yes, she completes me
on so many levels,

I've been through life's wringer,
but have made it back
to a place of happiness ...
         her love has saved me.

Alone

I do all the wrong things.
I say all the wrong things.
My insecurities are eating
away at the fiber of my being.

A boat out alone, adrift at sea.
It will probably continue until
the water pulls the boat down
into the ocean's murky depths.

      I will drown beneath
  a beautiful canopy of stars;
     it was meant to end,
        just like this ...

          alone.

The Cardinal

Crimson feathers of the cardinal
faze into scarlet.
Your slate black eyes and face
leave just a hint of mystery.
Your tiny orange bill
pecks aimlessly
at the bird feeder
hanging from the grey patio beam.

Shy little bird, inquisitive and insightful,
watching everything, ever so carefully.
You take seeds to your mate,
waiting on the power line,
hovering over the well-manicured lawns
of suburban utopia.

You carefully observe me
sitting on the lawn chair.
Your gut must tell you *'that guy's harmless,
his aura is wounded, but good.'*

And so, you leave your mate
sitting on the braided power lines
and awkwardly flutter over to
the windblown feeder, you eat well,
while we observe one another;
then as soon as you appeared
in your burst of red splendor,
you are gone again, like a fleeting thought,
or a soul that has flown.

My Life With You

The singing voices of birds
serenade us in the morning,
renewed days blossom
like a coreopsis in this photo garden,
strewn memories of us in simpler times:

>Down by the river in March,
holding hands with you.

>>By the Christmas lights
in December.

>>>Sunday Mass.

Your smile and perfume,
perfection,
linger like a kiss on my cheek
or a promise kept forever
at the altar.

Two Hearts

Hearts ablaze
soul on fire
dancing with her
in a dream
arms surround
in real time
the river flows
through this
little town
and here I am
the elder statesman
healed back into
optimum health
thanks to her
a treasured presence
in my life

the caress of her hand
the light in her eyes
that radiant smile
it gives me the focus
and drive to continue
navigating life's choppy
unpredictable waters

Love Poem

Tantalizing orange hibiscus skies,
you amaze me still —
infused into rose petal blossom hue
down by the wild grassy brush line.

The muddy river sincerely knows
my thoughts and dreams.
It knows of all those, gone before.

Years pass and birds serenade us.
Canadian geese communicate in honks
stuck in their rush hour flights,
lost in holding patterns
forming a heart like pattern
a kaleidoscope vision,
smoke rings spelling
out the words that read

"Love can mend
the broken hearted"

We are one spirit gathering
in a moving picture sky.

Life has begun
against the tapestry
of your diamond eyes.

I Still Think of Her, That Gulf of Mexico

The day expires, clutching on, but can't.
We're all just sauntering,
into winter's cool submission.

Most of the leaves
have relinquished lofty heights and are dead now.
They have fallen; mutely upon graves
and university lawns.

What would she say,
if she could see me now
in post middle age downfall?

That Gulf of Mexico, that mistress,
defining my life so clearly;
punctuated by her fathomed fist!

That Gulf of Mexico,
with her banshee scream,
in the form of hurricanes and tornados.

That Gulf of Mexico, I can swear, still,
that sometimes late at night,
she lulls me to sleep, like an infant
near her warm salty bosom.

And here in Midwest exile, am I,
deceiving her daily, and landlocked;
where nature stokes the fires
of creativity, where nature consumes
and imagination soars
more powerful than it ever could have been
if I would have stayed with her, my watery muse:

        That Gulf of Mexico!

Thursday Night

There's a calm
that's taken the night by surprise.

No sirens wailing from police cars.
No emergency vehicles on the prowl.

The dead are alone in their graves,
epitaphs writ their legacy known,
yet silent as the moss and fungi
reclaim their biological turf.

I sit here alone in this building
death hovering above
on the third floor,
students gone for the night,
the search for orthopedic supremacy
shall resume tomorrow.

I remain alone, an actor
upon this little stage of life,
in a little picturesque town,
      undeterred
awaiting my time to leave
and head on home,
where the woman I love
is lost to me, in the dark realm
of slumber and dreams.

Cryptic Thoughts

Who was that in the swirling mist of time,
knocking the shy moon off its pedestal?

Singing hymns in the blank garden
of wanton dead rose satire,
working with the lyrics of life,
the music in translucent song,
faded vision, weathered visage
of mountain hermit sage.

Were the ocean waves
caressing naked flesh and bone,
singing lullabies, like a mother,
      underneath
     the paleness
   of a canopy of stars?

Does that receding forest of cryptic myth
unravel questions of those
that have passed through,
     like ships
   on an uneventful night?

Manifest the Night

I want to be thin like bones,
glistening underneath
the motorcycle overpasses
of this small town,
howling in the bewitched midnight
of chloroform sleep.

I want to be a passenger
about to swerve,
dangerous upon the off ramp,
words more or less my friends,
taking this venom out from life
spatting into the pulse
of infectious moon,
dribble into a paper cup folly.

I want this to be the night
of calm, cool, & collected babble,
drifting aimlessly from sound rafters,
where the lost go to heal ...
where the wounded go to die.

The Ol' Mill

A line of trees basking
in the echoing silence
of the ragged Ol' Mill, clouds
assemble in their multitudes.

It's hard to believe this ramshackle place,
with its uneven floorboards,
and drafty windows,
could hold such lofty prices
and high clientele.

The walls creak as ghosts moan,
relics adorn flimsy shelves, barrels and tillers
from a bygone era.

Everything is overpriced,
the organic seed packets,
handcrafted flowerpots,
humorous bumper stickers,
fledgling fruit trees, etc.

Driving past the place,
I think about the rushing onyx river
lapping at the craggy riverbed.
      What secrets does it hide
        from those above?

Would that raging swollen river
like to take that paint peeled mill
into a watery grave?
Would that raging swollen river
like to pulverize that mill
into soggy kindling wood?

Or would it like to keep on slithering
on down in its cold methodical way?

The Dance

Dogwoods in bloom,
relinquished petals
plummet into lucid dreams
of yesterday.

Like ballerina's they swirl
dainty in complexity
carried by the gentle breeze
and kissed by the innocent
blues of skies that sing
to the world in serenade
Swan Lake Op. 20 ballet.

Dogwoods shedding their petals,
ballerinas at a loss,
damaged goods
upon touching down.

The earth shall use them
as things of beauty.
We shall crush them
under our calloused feet.

The 8th of April Eclipse

Was it Gods' birthday present to you?
God in the sky, and you, his little angel.

The darkest ring around the moon,
      his gift to you?

Sunshine on hiatus,
if only for under four minutes,

the eclipse will happen,
a sign of his return?

A second coming, on your birthday?

Mother dearest, angel in a sunless sky.
You left us too soon,
weeping underneath, a darkened sky,
      only at night,
    exposed in the light
  of the brightest moon.

Clear Blues

Clear blues of skies,
rebirth in her rebuttal,
owls have gone back
into their hidden slumber.
The birds and rabbits
are basking in the beauty
of-this Springtime vision.

My fingers are gliding across
    this keyboard. —

 Poems are being formed.
 They are taking shape
 for all the world to see.

Morning Songs

The white tails of gray rabbits
are bobbing in the morning sun.

The green, green grass is rain slicked
and Spring is here, yet again.

Birds shower us
with their inherited tunes.
It's not something they do
because they like us
rather than part of their DNA,
that forces them to sing a song
for all to hear.

Happy Anniversary

Nothing will ever change the fact
that I will love you for all eternity.

You have come into my life
when I was at my lowest
imaginable point.

You plucked me off the tiny apartment floor
when I was a rock and polished me
into the brightest diamond in the world.

I owe all I have to you.
You are an amazing woman,
my angel right here on planet earth.

I give my heart to you, completely.
My spirit is soaring because you
have taken a chance on me,
loved me, and have chosen to take
this life journey by my side.

I am forever indebted to you,
my angel here on earth.
My love is unmeasurable.

My heart, soul
and everything I have
I give unashamedly to you.

      I love you,
and only you, infinitely.

Surreal Montage

surreal montage
your red dress spins
in whirlwind bliss
wrapped within a dream

your gentle hands' caress
sends me into
the realm of ethereal splendor

were we not meant to roam this plain
and congregate amongst mere mortals?
were we once angels
banished from what was paradise?
that crimson tide
of effervescent duality
that aura locked within your blessed life

who shall tell us what the reality is?
the spontaneity of this moment,
of which we grasp

we are passing
through this lost and vast palace
oh this dying world
a mock run
wrapped in simple hopes,
that we are destined for
something much, much, more

Your Song

A diamond in the rough,
plucked with a calming hand,
from out of a smooth cosmos,
your presence is
what changed my entire existence,
that celestial star, polished and poised.

Yours is the voice of an exquisite angel
and while the intrepid galaxies unfurl,
I bask in phosphorus night
just listening to your song.

It's Summer Within Our Hearts

It's the depths of winter,
but summer lives within our hearts.
Her radiant smile,
bright blue eyes, wide as the sky,
hair flowing like a field of flowers
in the Netherlands.

She leaves me breathless,
with a kiss, always longing for more.
Always awaiting her
within a sacred dream;
and then it's reality —
that rosy hue on her cheeks
and delicate mouth.

My fair angel of the northern lights-
bask with me in the naked ocean tide,
underneath pristine moonbeams
and the pulsating rhythm
of us swimming together
through the mysteries
of unpredictable time.

Roses

The blood red roses
climb up the trellis
of infamy
into the complexities
of languid night.

Their callous thorns
are prickly and,
their petals taunt
and they share disinclination.

I am the artist,
the painter of cruel life.
My words aim to soothe
the roses in mid symphony.

I speak for the broken hearts
throughout the ages,
blood red roses given
love unrequited,
 their thorns penetrating raw emotion
and piercing flesh.

I am the dream relinquished.
The roses grow overwhelming
and cover what remains.

And Your Eyes Will See

In that still point
where early morning
shakes hands with the new day —
and the sleep is wiped away
and birds sing out a happy tune —
there is no mention
of this impending sadness.

    And then
before you know what hit you,
winter will bring his icy grasp
back into the forefront —
and your eyes
will finally see everything
        as infinite.

The Mere Thought of Us

Sing it in my ear again,
like the whispering wind.
Run your fingertips
across my aging visage,
and up my back, shoulders, arms.

I want to feel that spark again,
those flashes of electrical current flowing.
I want your voice slowly winding its way,
through the very valley of my soul.

      I want to feel your aura,
        so close again,
        sending shivers
          up my spine.

I want to feel our kiss
like we used to kiss,
      when it all began
and we fell so deeply in love
with the mere thought of us.

Secret Garden

Secret garden,
sacred ground, lake, and within
a spouting water feature,
memories captured —
the green park benches
keep our secrets, safe and sound,
tucked under satin sheets
of the cosmos
manicured lawns, lazy,
roam in green earthy hue.

Black rails and stone,
leading to the water's edge,
this is where we posed for pictures
on our wedding day
and paused for moments
of life's mysterious joy
and contemplation.

This is part of that grand veranda
     of our lives, now,
        so intertwined,
           for all time.

On Sundays

There's an elderly man
who attends Mass on Sunday.
He never ever misses it.
He looks just like Albert Einstein,
but dressed in cargo shorts
and a polo shirt instead.

He must know his time
is dwindling, slow winding time,
cruel to the body and hairline,
death takes loved ones one by one.
He watches them cross over that great divide,
a palace of golden rays and heaven obscured.

I have never seen him with
a relative or friend in tow,
and I wonder why.
I'm asking questions inside my mind —
   "Is it the miles that separate?"
   "Does his family not believe?"
   "Has death played a cruel hand?"

I always wanted to chat with him,
before or after Mass,
but haven't worked up
a good ice breaker as of yet.

His story must be so long and diverse.
I bet he's a wealth of knowledge and insight.

Nobody seems to notice his presence,
     in the second pew,
  large sad eyes in lament, yet
  with the silver lining of hope —
     remaining intact.

You Are My Destiny

Reflections in the water,
at pebble is tossed.
I was the naive young man once,
but time never slowed.
Those years did gallop
upon the knolls of dreaming,
they came like creaking bone doors.

Over a multitude of years,
they kept marching onward,
one by one the tin soldiers departed.

A glance back over my shoulder,
 the first refraction,
 the moon drenched-nights,
 stars bedazzled,
by that first kiss from you, to me;
and it's still burning like a comet
through the dazzling midnight sky.

And I will love you always,
because you are my destiny.

Your Wilderness

A table stands alone in the wilderness,
haphazard with wobbly aura,
moss is strewn over the top.
Vines climb the rickety legs.

There's a cardinal
perched on some brambles
that have come to lay claim
to heaven and earth
and everything in-between.

Cautious rabbits
and shy deer flee the scene.

This table will be sat at
    nevermore.

The friends of the forest
have forbidden that
from ever happening, again.

Crossing Over

Across the way there's a bridge
with the universe's name sprawled out.
It's a place of infinite wisdom.
The letters are carved into stars.

Automobiles drive slowly, drift past.
Lover's stroll underneath the bridge.
Lonely people saunter by;
they go unnoticed by anything or anyone.

There's no river of sighs
upon this frozen horizon;
just a sick feeling inside —
that the dream was never real
in the first place.

Just a mirage hidden away
in between the blood-letting
of an unfathomable endless night,
where the stars collapse
underneath their own cosmic tapestries,
of such painful implosions.

Sad Café

There's a place that some
unwillingly revisit in their lifespans.
        The Sad Cafe'
where the red walls weep shades of grey
and the photos are of ghosts
long gone from this mortal realm.
Where table tops and bar counters
are made of white and grey swirled marble.

      This is it;
this is where love goes to die,
      writhing in pain
on whiskey-stained cobblestone floors.

     This is where death is
    softly claiming your soul
one day at a time, until you bleed out,
  until there's nothing left to bleed
      at all.

Release

Keep steady on course.
The darkness closing in;
a ring toss into the abyss.

This game of life weighs heavy
upon my failing heart.
I cannot win at this game of life,
this dark cloud looming
from the day that I was born.

But soldier on now, I shall
and somehow will continue, to thrust —
my metaphorical bayonet,
into a cool jeweled night jostling with stars,
reel them out of the stratosphere,
toss them into the boat
allotted by God's good hand.

Love lays barren
on the ocean's twirling bottom.
It gasps flailing
its arms, its hand reaching,
bony fingers contorted like a spider's web;
the diamond has come undone
from its housing and is now lodged
in the coral reef of madness.

      It will never return.

The Transient Old Man

Numb in his heart,
he heads onwards
into the new day.
He feels broken by this world;
each beat of this drum
a reminder of nonstop pain:
pain in repetition,
pain that consumes his soul,
pain that destroys any faith
he had of a happy ever after.

Cabin in the Woods

The cabin in the woods
holds the keys to our fond memories.
We were so happy there.

I proposed to you
in the front left-hand corner
while you sat on the bed.
I snuck the wrapped up little box
behind my back.
I knelt before you
like a knight before his queen
asking your hand in marriage.
You shed a few tears of joy
whispering yes
and then once again,
a little louder, yes.

That was the happiest day of my life.
        Our auras
healed each other's broken heart
      and two became one
           for better or worse.

Lady of the Cosmos

Celestial lady of the mind's eye,
oh how I have loved you
since the calm dawn of time.

Flowers blooming in fields.
The cosmic flames swaying.
You're wading through,
back through the ocean tide,
back into my longing arms.
Oh how I yearn for you;
your love completes me.

The jade forests have passed on
through golden hues
of a subconscious dream,
passing through and beyond
the cherished night,
a myriad of stars,
phosphorescent and glistening
within lost orbits-

I can only see
the calm dawning of day,
as seen through your eyes,
      your voice echoing,
           'I am the cosmos.'

Beat Down in the Motor City

The travesty of sick roadside mission.

I am lost, wandering
in this beat down night.
Decrepit brow,
gave my last few dollars
to a homeless man,
outside of Comerica Park.

His cardboard sign,
written in neat black sharpie pen,
"lack of a post-retirement pension"

The system left him out of luck
on the mean streets of Detroit.
Oh that mad, mean motor city
sure to chew you up and spit you out
onto the grimy sidewalk.

It could happen to anyone.
It could happen to me,
and it could happen to you.

When Life Was Our Song

And when the weight of this golden day
drags your bones nearer
into the fragrant weariness of mother earth;
when your smile has worn thin and brittle
with the red years of wisdom,
latent, black and withering away
in the mist strewn tomb
where no mortal weeps,
where no bird's tweet.

And yet, the isolated caw of the raven,
blue black and cradled within the soft pyre
of mocking architect-leaves
plummets into the cobbles
of our dreaming brows and snowy bones,
collecting the years underneath the mystery
of what was us-in the times where fleshy prisons
held us coherent into the abyss
of the real world, and where our song
could be heard, loud and clear
for all the world to hear again and again.

From the Ashes

Conflicted by the yin & yang of life,
the light and the dark
the good and evil,
clouds and crows circling above,
mocking and training in their laughter
and haunted allure.

Bask with me this one moment,
upon the thistle path of dream times
warm in the essence of lost mornings;
a plume of steam listless and rising,
     from a coffee mug,
like a phoenix from the ashes.

AUTHOR PROFILE:

Wayne Russell is a poet, originally from central Florida, he is an aspiring rhythm guitar player, and university taught photographer; he also loves to write song lyrics. He is a 2006 AA holder in Graphic Design and graduated from the Universal College of Learning in Palmerston North, New Zealand. He has been writing poetry, short stories, and novellas for many decades. Wayne was first published in the Quill Poetry Anthology back when he was a high school senior in 1989.

Since the dawning of the internet craze that swept the globe in the mid to late 1990's; Wayne has taken full advantage of this, and put away his postage stamps and envelopes, in favor of emailed creative writing endeavors. After many rejections, Waynes' poetry, photography, and short stories started to gain recognition by the editorial staff at mainly at the Poets' Espresso Review, Rye Whiskey Review, as well as Jotters Utd circa 2006, in which Wayne is both indebted too, and proud to call them "his muse catalysis."

Wayne has received a 'Best of the Net' nomination and a 'Pushcart Prize' nomination. His 1st book, "Where Angels Fear" was published by Guarilia Genius Press in 2020. His 2nd book "Splinter of the Moon" was published by Silver Bow Publishing 2024. "Waves of Lucidity" is Wayne's third book of poetry. He currently resides in Southeast Ohio with his beloved wife.

www.ingramcontent.com/pod-product-compliance
Lightning Source LLC
Chambersburg PA
CBHW052205070526
44585CB00017B/2082